Xenophobe's Guide to The English

Antony Miall
David Milsted

〇
Oval Books

Published by Oval Books
335 Kennington Road
London SE11 4QE

Telephone: (0171) 582 7123
Fax: (0171) 582 1022
E-mail: info@ovalbooks.com

First published by Ravette Publishing.
This edition published by Oval Books.

First edition 1993
Updated 1994
Reprinted 1995, 1996, 1997, 1998
Revised edition 1999

Series Editor – Anne Tauté

Cover designer – Jim Wire, Quantum
Printer – Caledonian International Ltd

Contents

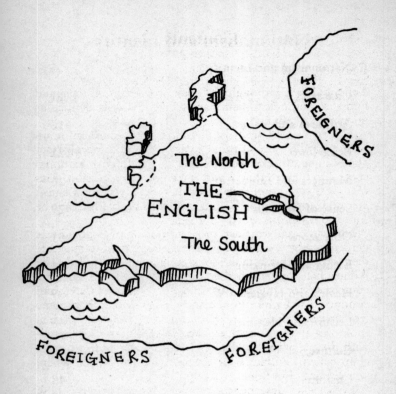

'The English have a natural distrust of the unfamiliar and nowhere is this more clearly seen than in their attitude to the geography of their own country.'

The English population is 48 million (compared with 5 million Scots, 15 million Dutch, 39 million Spanish, 58 million French, 81 million Germans and 268 million Americans).

Nationalism and Identity

Forewarned

Xenophobia*, although a Greek word, has its spiritual home in the English dictionary where it is drily defined as an 'abstract' noun.

This is misleading. It is, in fact, a very 'common' noun – an everyday sort of noun really, with nothing abstract about it at all. For xenophobia is the English national sport – England's most enduring cultural expression. And there is a very good reason for that. As far as the English are concerned, all of life's greatest problems can be summed up in one word – foreigners.

Nine hundred years ago the last invasion of England was perpetrated by the Normans. They settled, tried to integrate themselves with the indigenous population and failed. The indigenous population then, as now, displayed an utter contempt for them not merely because they had conquered but more importantly because they had come from abroad. However, eventually Anglo-Saxon women took pity on the poor things and started marrying them – with the inevitable civilising effect. You wouldn't trust a chap called Guillaume de Bohun, but you know where you are with Bill Bone.

Even today descendants of those Normans who think to impress with a throw-away remark about their families having 'come over with the Conqueror' find themselves on the receiving end of the sort of English frost normally reserved for someone who has let off in a lift.

The real English deal with them as they dealt with the Romans, the Phoenicians, the Celts, Jutes, Saxons and, more recently, every other nation on earth (especially the French) – with polite but firm disdain.

*In fact the English prefer 'xenolipi' (pity for foreigners) but both words, being foreign in origin, are of limited pertinence in any case.

This is what you are up against. It is useless to imagine that you can succeed where so many have failed. But since it is the proudest English boast that they cannot begin to understand foreigners, it would be gratifying to steal a march on them by beginning to understand *them*.

How They See Themselves

Despite having the second largest prison population in western Europe, the English insist that they are amongst the most, if not *the* most, civilized nations in the world. Civilized not so much in terms of culture, perhaps, as in social behaviour. They consider themselves to be law abiding, courteous, tolerant, decent, generous, gallant, steadfast and fair. They also take pride in their self-deprecatory sense of humour which they see as the ultimate proof of their magnanimity.

Believing themselves superior to all other nations, they are also convinced that all other nations secretly know that they are. In a perfect world, the English suspect everyone would be more like them.

Geography reinforces this belief as the inhabitants look out to the sea all around them from the fastness of their 'tight little island'. Nobody would ever question the aptness of the newspaper report: 'Fog in the Channel – Continent cut off.'

The English are convinced that the best things in life originated in England or have been improved there. Even the weather, though it may not be pleasant, is far more interesting than anyone else's and is always full of surprises. '...this scept'rd isle...This precious stone set in the silver sea...this England.' Few people could explain all Shakespeare's allusions, but they know exactly what he meant by them. To its natives, England isn't so much a place as a state of mind, an attitude to life and the universe that puts both firmly in their place.

How They Think Others See Them

By and large, the English do not really care how the rest of the world sees them. They are convinced, with some justification, that no-one really understands them. This is not a cause for national concern, since they do not want to be understood (feeling it to be an invasion of their privacy) and work quite hard to remain obscure.

The English are used to being seen as stereotypes and prefer it that way. They are aware that many foreigners see them as being hopelessly wedded to the past. And they don't mind in the least that England is seen as peopled by amateur detectives, football hooligans, silly-ass nobility and suitably servile peasants, all meeting for a pint of warm beer at an ancient pub.

How Others Actually See Them

To outsiders the English are intellectually impenetrable. They express little emotion, their culinary appreciation is incomprehensible and the pleasures of life seem to pass them by as they revel in discomfort and self-denial. They are seen as hidebound, prejudiced and unco-operative – a nation largely unmoved by developments in the world around them, who prefer to live in a land of BBC costume dramas walled in by the White Cliffs of Dover, roofed over by perpetually grey skies, fortified with beer and roast beef and firmly underpinned with imperishable corsetry.

How They Would Like to be Seen

Although it is impossible for the English to appear to care what others think of them, deep down they would like to be loved and appreciated for what they see as the sterling qualities they possess. These qualities, which they bring selflessly to the world forum, include a reflex action which leads them to champion the underdog and treat persecutors with a firm hand, absolute truthfulness and a commitment never to break a promise or to go back on one's word. Foreigners are expected to understand that if an Englishman hasn't kept his word, there is a very good reason for it – up to and including enlightened (i.e. naked) self-interest.

If possible, try to find it in your heart to be charitable about these and other beliefs, even if you are convinced they are delusions. Aside from anything else, the moment you disagree, most English will take your side and agree with you. Respect for the underdog, you see.

How They See Others

The English have a natural distrust of the unfamiliar and nowhere is this more clearly seen than in their attitude to the geography of their own country.

Since time immemorial there has been a North-South divide in England. To the Southerner, civilization ends somewhere around the Watford Gap (just north of London). Beyond that point, he believes, the inhabitants are all ruddier in complexion, more hirsute and blunt to the point of rudeness. These traits he generously puts down to the cooler climate.

In the North they frighten their children to sleep with tales of the deviousness of the inhabitants 'down South'. They point to their softness, their mucked-about food and their airy-fairiness on all matters of real importance. Nevertheless, *any* English person no matter how soft or hairy, is entitled to special treatment as, to a lesser extent, are the inhabitants of those countries which represent the English conscience – once the Empire, now the shrinking Commonwealth.

When it comes to their neighbours in the British Isles, the English are in absolutely no doubt as to their own predominance. This they see as no petty prejudice but rather as a scientific observation. The Irish are a nuisance and feckless to boot; the Scots are clever but too careful with money, and the Welsh are simply not to be trusted. Not even by the Scots and the Irish.

However, the Irish, Welsh and Scots should take heart. For most English they are not quite as objectionable as their cousins across the Channel. They should also remember that 'foreign-ness' for the English starts to a certain extent at the end of their own street.

The rest of the world the English see as a playground: a series of interlocking peoples, customs and cultures all of which can be enjoyed, used, or discarded as the whim takes them. Their own experience has taught them to expect the worst and be pleasantly surprised if it doesn't happen, slightly gratified with their own sensible misgivings if it does.

Strangely, the English do like many individuals who are foreign. They generally know at least one 'foreigner' who is almost 'one of us'. But there are very few nations they either trust or take seriously.

The French and the English have been sparring partners for so long that the English have developed a kind of love-hate relationship with them. The English love France: they love its food and wine and thoroughly approve of its climate. There is a subconscious historical belief that the French have no right to be living in France at all, to the extent that thousands of the English try annually to turn certain areas of France into little corners of Surrey.

The French themselves are perceived as a bit too excitable for any people with ambitions on the world stage. It is thought that a few more decades of gradual English influence would improve them no end.

With the Germans the English are less equivocal.

Germans are regimented, far too serious, and inclined to bullying; they have not even the saving grace of culinary skill. On the other hand, Italians are too emotional; the Spanish cruel to bulls; the Russians, gloomy; the Dutch solid (but sensible); Scandinavians, Belgians and Swiss, dull. All oriental peoples are inscrutable and dangerous.

The Indians are in a special category: they play cricket.

Special Relationships

There are one or two favoured nations with whom the English feel a special affinity.

They have close ties with the Australians, in spite of their disconcerting lack of restraint, and the Canadians, although they are seen as a people embittered by permanent snow and being too close to America.

They like Americans and in many ways would probably like them even more if only they didn't insist on being quite so... well... *American*. The English regard Americans as English people who turned into something else as the result of an unfortunate misunderstanding, and who would be a lot happier if only they had the sense to turn back again. Then they would start talking Proper English.

English viewers watch participants on American television talk shows with fascinated disbelief and blame falling standards in their own cultural life on American influence.

In the final analysis, however, they need to maintain good relations with the Americans for the sake of commercial and political advantage. But this does not stop them from comparing the two countries to America's disadvantage. They are older, after all.

Character

Two Faces

It is a favourite English saying that 'there are two sides to everything'. This platitude is most usually trotted out in reference to discussions and disagreements. But of all the things that have two sides none is more clearly two-sided than the English character.

On the surface the English usually appear reserved and unflappable. With their buttoned-up emotions and their composure completely in place, they present a reassuring consistency to each other and the world at large. Underneath, however, they seethe with a kind of primitive violence which they have never been able completely to control. This 'dark' side of their characters is something they try to ignore and do their best to cover up. From birth English children are taught to dissemble, to conceal any dangerously excessive tendencies and thereby to avoid giving offence. Watching their elders, they see that they very often say one thing and do another. When they question this, they are told to 'do as I say, not as I do'. Appearance is all. Very soon the little Januses get the hang of it and grow up with the two faces of their English character well established, their masks securely in place.

But when unruly passions rise and disguises slip they become confused. The English have no talent for handling passion. When confronted by it in others, they will mostly duck down behind their newspapers in embarrassment, and pretend that it isn't happening. Extreme outbursts, such as football hooliganism or road rage, will elicit a chorus of indignation. Even though such behaviour is quite common and quite in character, it is still perceived as 'un-English'.

The truth is that deep down the English are just as capable of deception, rudeness, violence and sheer bad behaviour as anybody, but they seldom appear to be. It is this opaqueness which is their chief characteristic and one which paradoxically makes this apparently predictable race so very unpredictable.

The English can admire something without enjoying it or enjoy something they suspect is fundamentally reprehensible. You can never be sure which stance they are going to take – the reassuringly reasonable, or the wildly irrational. So, at a checkout, clutching two items, you may find someone with a trolley-load standing back to let you go first, yet in a crowded pub you may find the same person barging in front of you to get to the bar. Climate, too, has a lot to do with it. Heat waves bring out the beast in the English. Cold and drizzle calm them down.

The interplay between these two facets of the English character prompts the most common criticism of them – that they are hypocrites. They certainly appear to be but appearances can be deceptive. They just believe that, like everything else, even the truth has two sides.

Contradictory Desires

Two equally fundamental but contradictory English characteristics are a love of continuity and a yearning for change. In the English character these two opposite desires vie with each other constantly, which produces some curious behaviour patterns and several characteristics most usually observed in the classic split personality.

Although they like to think of themselves and their way of life as being thoroughly consistent, this is an illusion. They are, in fact, in a constant state of flux. With the pursuit of change in the ascendant, the English will still cling to aspects of their past as timid workmen cling to their ladders. Whilst appearing to be heading for a bright new tomorrow, their alter egos are frantically trying to get back to a cosy yesterday. So at the same time as the government deliberate endlessly about spending public money on a winter weather allowance for the elderly or tinker about with pay increases for nurses, they joyfully give the nod to a budget of £11.2m for the restoration of the Albert Memorial.

Tradition

The English are a deeply nostalgic people and value customs and traditions above almost everything. It does not seem to matter just where traditions have come from or why they have survived. They are traditions, and that is enough for them.

Tradition, to the English, represents continuity, which must be preserved at all costs. It gives them a sense of permanence in an age of change. Like a well-worn jersey with holes in the sleeves, it's the comfort of the familiar.

By extension, the word 'traditional' implies that something has stood the test of time on its own merits and should be preserved – red pillar boxes, duffel coats, marmalade, the August Bank Holiday, the pint, privet hedges, Wembley Stadium, Wellington boots.

Because their past was so infinitely more glamorous than their present, the English cling to it tenaciously. It's a matter of preserving something not for what it is now, but for what it was once.

Their public and private ceremonies are full of people (mainly men) walking backwards, having doors ceremoniously slammed in their faces, parading in gilded coaches, and wearing embroidered aprons, stockings and tabards. On state occasions several large bodies of men from mainly aristocratic families (normally confined to barracks) meet in full dress uniform on a large parade ground and do quite a lot of marching about and looking fierce in front of the current monarch. In this they are accompanied by noisy wind bands playing mostly German music.

Eighteenth-century wigs are still worn by the judiciary

and nobody smirks. Members of Parliament making a point of order in the House of Commons wear a collapsible opera hat and nobody sniggers. It must be right. It's always been like that. It's traditional.

Moderation

Moderation – a treasured ideal – means a lot to the English. Their respect for it is reflected in their shared dislike of any person who 'goes too far'. At the first suspicion of any situation having 'gone too far' they start back-peddling frantically in order to settle down to that most desirable mean – the state of mediocrity in which the English feel most comfortable most of the time.

Going too far in behavioural terms covers displaying an excess of emotion, getting hopelessly drunk or cracking off-colour jokes and then laughing at them noisily. Beyond the pale* altogether is the man or woman who regales one with his or her titles or qualifications. The only acceptable place to air these is on an envelope.

The English do not like to make a scene in public. Anyone who does so is automatically in the wrong, even if they are actually in the right. The whole business of making a fuss has its own vocabulary: guilty parties being accused of creating a 'hoo-hah', a 'hullaballoo', a 'to do', a 'palaver', a 'kerfuffle', a 'song and dance' – all of which are seen as socially undesirable.

To the English the proper way to behave in almost all situations is to display a languid indifference to almost everything, though one may be fuming underneath. Even in affairs of the heart, it is considered unseemly to show one's feelings except behind closed doors, and even then with moderation.

* Not a reference to a fence, but an area of land in Ireland (The Pale) ruled by the 'civilized' English, beyond which roamed the 'barbaric' native Irish.

Paradoxically, the sentence 'This time you/he/she/they have gone too far' is the unmistakable prelude to a great deal of immoderate behaviour on the part of the speaker who will then undoubtedly go too far him- or herself.

Individualism

The English have a well-developed sense of individual personal freedom which at its most dogmatic says: 'I will obey the law only because I choose to do so. And only then because it either makes sense or there's no good reason not to – given that I am the ultimate judge of both conditions.'

Whoever called the English 'the Island Race' only got it half right. Every English person is his or her own island. Only wars unite the English. Over the years they've become quite good at them, but natural modesty demands they should always look like losing until just before the end. It makes victory that much sweeter and really annoys the loser.

The English are fond of their rights, including the right to privacy and the right to preserve one's personal space. This is an area surrounding each individual, which it is not good manners to invade. People will leave a step between them and the next person on an escalator even when it's crammed, or a vacant seat between them and their neighbour in the cinema. This has nothing to do with a morbid fear of body odour, it is more an extension of the 'an Englishman's home is his castle' belief. Think of it as an invisible moat. Learn to shake hands at long distance.

Attitudes and Values

The English are governed by a simple set of attitudes and values to which everyone pays lip service, whether they believe in them or not. There is, however, one exception to this rule, and that is:

Common Sense

Common sense is central to the English attitude to almost everything in life. It is common sense to carry an umbrella in case of rain. It is common sense not to sit on cold stone (which bestows haemorrhoids). It is common sense to wear clean underwear in case one is run over and taken to hospital.

In fact, it is common sense and thoroughly English never to be wrong-footed in any way. To fall foul of changing circumstances is inexcusable. One should 'be prepared' at all times. Every plan for an outdoor event will have its indoor alternative in case 'the worst comes to the worst'. Even their accounting systems have a line for 'contingencies'. The fact that when they come to business meetings they are often less prepared than any other nation does not deter them from believing that common sense will prevail.

It is common sense that sets the English apart: they may look silly in their plastic macs on the Riviera, but the last laugh will be on those who mock them if the Mistral comes early.

A Good Sport

If an English man or woman refers to you as 'a good sport', you will know that you have really arrived. For to them it is a qualification normally never awarded to a foreigner and by no means within the grasp of all the

English.

The term is not exclusively a sporting one. It describes the sort of behaviour both on and off the playing field that characterises everything the English really respect. In all physical trials, the good sport will play without having been seen to practise too hard and will, ideally, win from innate superiority. He or she will then be dismissive of their victory and magnanimous towards the loser.

It goes without saying that the good sport will also be a good loser. There will be no arguing with umpires or outward signs of disappointment. On the contrary, a remark such as "The best man won!" tossed airily to all and sundry, and never through clenched teeth, is obligatory even in the face of crushing defeat.

This does not really fool anyone, for the English are fiercely competitive especially in matters sporting. They would rather be crossed in love than beaten on the tennis courts, but to let it be seen would be going too far.

A Puritan Streak

In general, the English do not take soul-searching seriously, and are one of the least introspective of all races. This doesn't prevent them from brooding every now and then, usually after a major sporting defeat or several weeks' continual rain.

What they do have is a strong puritan streak which runs so deep that few are aware of it. Their restrictive licensing laws are a case in point. Even though they have now been relaxed, the English still fundamentally believe that it is wrong to indulge yourself 24 hours a day.

Having debated for decades whether or not to have a national lottery, they now argue about whether or not the prizes should be quite so gargantuan: they feel there is something faintly indecent about anyone being able to win such huge amounts of money all at once.

They worry about moral standards on television and have a nine o'clock watershed after which the children ought not to be around to be corrupted by explicit sex, bad language and violence – all the things, in fact, that their 13-year-olds get up to in the playground.

English Puritanism is best expressed in the belief that if something is nasty it must be good for you. There can be no other explanation for the existence of tapioca pudding.

Inventiveness

The English are endlessly resourceful and inventive, but rarely profit from their inventions. Inventors in their garden sheds turning out gadgets tend to be almost exclusively male, their ingenuity far surpassing their business sense. Often perceiving needs in daily life which have gone unobserved by the rest of their compatriots, they will beaver away, creating such indispensable items as the perfect egg boiler, the self-creasing trouser or a little ladder to let the spider out of the bath. Occasionally, though, they will come up with something with real promise like the hovercraft which will then be ignored by their countrymen and taken up by foreigners.

Clubbability

Belonging is important to the English. Individuality is all very well, and in some cases commendable, but on the whole being part of a team is their preferred situation and they are never happier than when they are surrounded by a group of people with whom they either have, or affect to have, everything in common. This mutual tacit approval reassures them and stifles any feelings of insecurity.

For this reason English life is riddled with clubs and societies. On the surface many of these appear to have a

particular scientific or academic purpose – The Jane
Austen Society, The Institute for Psychical Research, The
Sealed Knot (for recreating famous battles of the Civil
War period), the Society for the Prevention of Inadvertent
Transatlanticisms (SPIT). Others are run for and by
collectors – The Ephemera Society, The Jigsaw Society,
The British Button Society. But whatever their avowed
purpose, all English clubs are primarily just social group-
ings in which the members take comfort in being able to
relate to each other – without in fact having to do so.

Class

This urge for togetherness manifests itself in a devotion to
the class system which, though constantly under threat,
remains stubbornly central to the way of life of vast numbers of the English. For them its importance can hardly
be overrated and it should never be dismissed. For
English men and women, their class is the largest club to
which they belong.

This they do by manoeuvring themselves into cliques in
whose company they feel comfortable. Once there they
adopt mutually exclusive fashions of all kinds and nurture a kind of phobia about other groupings to which
they do not belong.

English tradition demands the existence of three classes.
Once upon a time these equated to the old groupings of
aristocracy, merchants and workers. However, with the
irresistible rise of the merchant or middle class, the aristocracy and workers were squeezed out of the frame and
the middle class turned its attention to dividing itself into
an upper, middle and lower class.

However, in the last quarter of the 20th century the
whole of society has shifted once again and transformed
itself into the five alphabetical groups recognised by
marketeers. The upper echelons are ABs and the middle,

BCs. The lower stratum divides again into Ds and Es. The Ds consider themselves to be underprivileged and hold everyone else in contempt. The Es are the underclass and thus usually left out of the picture. The overwhelming majority of the indigenous English are, in fact, BCs. In this group, the Cs constantly aspire to be Bs, and the nightmare for Bs is to become Cs.

Because of this, the BCs can never relax. They are conscious that in every aspect of life they should project the 'right' image – one based on their perception of what others think of them. This involves what they wear, what they say, what they eat and drink, where they live and with whom they are seen.

Although they firmly assert that greater social mobility is desirable, they generally believe one should always marry within one's own peer group. It saves arguments over whether china ducks on the wall are a good or bad thing, or whether or not to use the fish knives.

Placing Each Other

Nothing upsets an Englishman so much as not being able to 'place' another – or worse, making a mistake about another's social position. If they are not totally sure, they will resort to a fiendish series of social tests.

Accents can instantly place an individual. A regional drawl is no longer necessarily a fatal flaw but what used to be called an 'Oxford' accent or 'BBC' pronunciation will still give advantage to someone with it.

Probably even more telling than vowel sounds is vocabulary. People will distinguish one another by those who refer to 'lunch' not 'dinner' at lunchtime, have a 'pudding' not a 'sweet' or 'afters'; sit in the 'sitting room' rather than the 'lounge', on a 'sofa' not a 'settee', or go to the 'loo' not the 'toilet'. There are a myriad such distinctions which allow one group to disparage the other.

Manners at mealtimes provide yet another opportunity for categorising. The big divide comes in the method of holding one's knife and fork. Some hold both firmly with the handles covered by the palm. Others hold them loosely like drumsticks with the handles sticking up. Eating peas in either pose is something which needs watching.

Even the consumption of soup can define the diner, some following an ancient maritime tradition and tipping the bowl away to avoid the soup spilling on to their laps in the event of a swell.

Behaviour

Keeping a Stiff Upper Lip

This characteristic pose involves keeping the head held high (pride), the upper lip stiff (to avoid the visible tremble which betrays emotion) and the best foot forward (determination). In this position, conversation is difficult and intimacy of any kind almost impossible. But it portrays the presence of that attribute which the English think they are expected to project – absolute self-control.

There are, however, specific occasions on which it is considered proper to show one's feelings openly, for instance, sporting events, funerals or welcoming home someone thought to have been dead. At times like these it is permissible to show a certain amount of emotion, but only if one looks suitably embarrassed afterwards.

Minding Your Own Business

They also believe in minding their own business. With such a complex set of tribal mores in existence, it is too easy to upset someone unknowingly. Few foreigners understand to what extent the English are determined to mind their own business.

The queue is one of the few places where the English are allowed to talk to each other without having been formally introduced. The others are when taking the dog for a walk, or any serious catastrophe, like an accident. However it is firmly understood that any friendships made remain outside with the dogs or stop when rescue arrives. Being trapped with an English person in, say, a tunnel in an underground train, might result in community singing, even the exchange of confidences – but it is not an invitation to a more permanent intimacy.

Stoicism

It is reported that, during the Battle of Waterloo, the Duke of Wellington saw that one of his commanders had been wounded by cannon fire. 'Good God, sir,' he said. 'I believe your leg's been shot off.' 'Good God, sir,' the General replied, 'I believe it has.' Only then did the gallant gentleman allow himself to fall off his horse.

Stoicism, the capacity to greet life's vicissitudes with cheerful calm, is an essential ingredient of Englishness. It is not the sort of unfeeling woodenness implied by the expression 'stiff upper lip', nor is it oriental fatalism or Scandinavian gloom. It is the attitude to life best expressed in Rudyard Kipling's *If*, which the English have voted their most popular poem:

If you can meet with triumph and disaster,
And treat those two impostors just the same.

The English, who suspect that all foreigners tend to over-react and 'make a meal of things', will warm to you instantly if you display understated good humour in the face of adversity. A typical English stoic is the circus worker who had his arm bitten off by a tiger. On admission to hospital he was asked if he was allergic to anything. 'Only tigers,' he said.

Families

The English family is a grouping of closely related people who like to indulge their passions for individuality and privacy in company.

Families allow the English the luxury of behaving as they want to, and not as they think they should. However, annual holidays apart, they do not tend to spend much time together. Once the tiresome business of childhood is over, they set out on life's journey largely unhampered by considerations of siblings or parents.

The 'traditional English family' – father at work, married to mother at home, with 2.4 children – is far from the norm: 30% of parents are unmarried, 10% of children are raised by a single parent (of whom 10% are men), and two in five marriages end in divorce. Two-thirds of divorced people remarry, and two-thirds of people who divorce their second spouse go on to marry a third. Most then settle down, possibly through sheer exhaustion.

Many couples seek marriage counselling and sometimes this works because, being English, their resentment at being bossed about by some do-gooding busybody finally makes them relate to each other.

Children

The English have a Royal Society for Prevention of Cruelty to Animals (that is, under Crown patronage), and a Royal Society for the Protection of Birds, yet there is only a *National* Society for the Prevention of Cruelty to Children. Clearly it is thought unfair to saddle the royal family with the responsibility for anyone else's offspring.

Parents seem to find their children a problem. At Christmas and on birthdays they shower them with presents (anything for peace) and at other times they just try to contain them, preferring to leave their upbringing to others or letting them rear themselves.

For children, an English childhood is something to be got over as quickly as possible and then looked back on with misty-eyed fondness. To be an English grown-up is reckoned a great and glorious thing: it carries much less responsibility than being an English child.

Elders

By and large, the English find their elderly awkward. They are often ignored by their families and, funds permitting, banged up in twilight homes. Every so often they will be visited by their relations who check that they are basically healthy and happy and that the security systems are in good order.

With their children at school and their old people out of harm's way, they can get on with the real business of life, with which, they believe, neither youth nor old age is equipped to cope.

Eccentrics

To the rest of the world the entire English race is eccentric. To the English themselves, the concept of eccentricity is a useful way of coping with the problem of anti-social behaviour in one of their own kind. So, to a certain extent, the English cultivate the idea of eccentricity as agreeable and even admirable.

The phenomenon of the eccentric does exist in its own right, though money and status help. The wealthier or

24

more famous you are, the more likely you are to be regarded as eccentric rather than peculiar, barmy, or barking mad. It is all a question of scale. Thus non-threatening dotty behaviour, such as Lord Berners' penchant for dyeing his flock of doves in different colours so that they formed a rainbow when they flew into the air, was met with affectionate indulgence. He was, after all, a Lord. Similarly, the residents of a suburban street will put up with the antics of an elderly bag-lady residing in a parked car if she is known to have been a famous concert pianist.

Eccentrics are excused *de facto* from many of the conventions of correct English conduct. They are living proof that the rules can be broken. However, they are only tolerated if they are apparently unaware of their own eccentricity.

Racial Minorities

As the result of having had an empire, the English are used to having a multi-racial society and usually accord their immigrants just enough civility to make their lives bearable. In many ways they are treated rather like English children. That is to say, they are seen but not heard.

Anyone visiting a large English town cannot fail to be aware of the rich mix of nationalities. Around 3.2 million (6%) of the UK population belong to ethnic minorities, and of these 20% live in London.

Immigrants are generally welcomed if they have something valuable to offer the community. But the English do not see why any immigrant should expect to become part of the community within a matter of days, months or even years of their arrival. Any such ease of assimilation would, after all, make a mockery of the thousands of years it has taken to produce England and the English proper.

The obnoxious behaviour of racial extremists appals

the native majority, though not as much as it appals the target minority. The English are basically a tolerant people, their attitude to minority groups being cool, if condescending. Being cliquey themselves, they do not feel unduly threatened by others forming groups within their culture, provided they don't impinge. A racial minority will usually only attract dislike when it shows signs of losing its underdog status.

Manners and Etiquette

It is generally believed that the English are more formal than they really are. In fact, in day-to-day contact with each other they are less inclined to formality than the French or the Germans.

They are happy to show affection or enthusiasm for one another when they are feeling socially secure. On the other hand English group greetings are incredibly polite and can last for such a long time that everyone forgets each other's name. When this happens the whole business is likely to begin again.

First names are commonly used among colleagues, and the American habit of using these on the telephone even before the names have met is now widespread.

The custom of men deferring to women is somewhat on the wane, thanks to the strenuous efforts of the apostles of political correctness who see it more as condescension than consideration. You will, however, probably still get away with opening a door or giving up a seat for all but the most strident of feminists. But it is no longer de rigueur to jump to your feet when a woman enters the room, whether or not there are enough chairs.

Do Not Touch

However informal they are in their manner or address, when it comes to physical contact, the English are still deeply reserved.

They are not a tactile people. They do shake hands with each other, but as little as possible. With acquaintances once in a lifetime is often considered enough. Any more and one runs the risk of behaving like a life insurance salesman. The preferred English handshake is a brief, vigorous affair with no hint of lingering. The standard greeting "How do you do" and the reply "How do you do" signal the end of the ritual and hands should be crisply withdrawn from contact. Foreigners who assume that 'How do you do' comes with a built-in question mark and respond accordingly become socially isolated.

The bluff hearty handshake beloved by men with muscular fingers is less a greeting than a trial of strength. The winner is allowed to clap the loser firmly on the back. Most Englishmen never hug or (perish the thought) kiss other men. They leave that to football players and foreigners. Women may kiss on one or both cheeks; if they do, the miss-kiss is preferred – the kisser making a kissing gesture with appropriate sound-effects in the air in the general region of the recipient's ear.

Men may also kiss women in greeting, but only on the cheek. Trying to get a kiss on both cheeks can be risky as most women only expect the one, do not turn their heads for the second and receive it full frontally, which can result in the worst being feared – i.e. that it was an intentional ploy – an osculatory rape.

Farewells are more varied than greetings and mean as little. For example, the once down-market 'see you' now becoming popular in politer society, means nothing of the sort. In fact, it is more likely to be used when someone is leaving on a two-year snowflake monitoring expedition in the Antarctic. Or setting off on a mission from which

There Will Be No Return.

In public places, the English make strenuous efforts not to touch strangers even by accident. If such an accident should occur, apologies are fulsome but should never be used as an excuse for further conversation. On crowded public transport where it is sometimes unavoidable, physical contact with a stranger is permitted, but in such circumstances, eye contact should be avoided at all costs.

Intimacy between consenting adults is recognised as involving more touching. But this takes place in private, usually with the lights out.

Please and Thank You

English children have their own particular catechism of accepted conduct to learn. The first rule they come across at an early age is the importance of saying 'Please' and 'Thank you'. Supplication, gratitude and, most important of all, apology are central to English social intercourse, which is why English people seem to express them endlessly, as if to the hard of hearing.

'Excuse me', 'I'm sorry to tell you...', 'I'm afraid that...' when apology, regret or fear have nothing to do with it are all forms of social lubrication which spare others' feelings and make life on an small, overcrowded island a little easier.

It is difficult for outsiders to learn how to wield the vocabulary necessary, but the starting point is to understand that it is almost impossible linguistically to be over-grateful, over-apologetic or over-polite when it comes to the point. Thus, the English man or woman whose toe you tread on will be 'so sorry' presumably for not having had the offending digit amputated earlier. He or she will thank you 'so much' when you stop treading on it or, if you do not, ask you to with a routine of pleases and thank yous that would last any other national half a lifetime. It's just the English way.

A lack of profusion in the gratitude or apology department will certainly land anyone in such a situation in the 'not very nice' camp from which there is little chance of escape.

Sense of Humour

The English have an island culture – quirky and self-contained. Much of their humour is highly sophisticated and elusively subtle. Like the will-o'-the-wisp, it often refuses to be caught and examined and just when you think you have cracked it, you realise that you have been duped once again. For example:

Two men are reading their newspapers when one says: 'It says here there's a fellow in Devon who plays his cello to the seals.' 'Oh really', says the other. 'Yes', says the first, 'Of course, they don't take a blind bit of notice.'

Since the English rarely say what they mean and tend towards reticence and understatement, their humour is partly based on an exaggeration of this facet of their own character. So, while in conversation they avoid truths which might lead to confrontation, in their humour they mock that avoidance. For instance:

At dinner in a great country house, one of the guests drinks too much wine, and slumps across the table. The host rings for the butler and says: 'Smithers, could you please prepare a room. This gentleman has kindly consented to stay the night.'

Tact and diplomacy are held up to ridicule in a way which would appear to give the lie to all that the English actually seem to hold dear. Thus in a popular television situation comedy, *Yes, Minister*, you are encouraged to laugh at the elaborate verbal subterfuge of the civil servant who can turn black into white and convince everyone that they are one and the same thing.

Comedy also celebrates weakness and vulnerability with self-deprecation as a way of establishing superiority. Many of their successful sitcoms are about people who are failures in society's eyes. It is not the failure that makes the comedy. It is the heroic struggle for success.

For instance, in the sitcom *Dad's Army*, the bumbling amateurism of an elderly group of men formed as a Home Guard unit to protect their country in World War II is amusing not only because they believe themselves to be invincible and more than a match for the ruthless professionalism of the Germans, but because the audience believes the same.

The English are so secure in their self-regard that they can happily poke fun at themselves. Complain about some aspect of English life that is quite awful and they will gleefully tell stories of trains that never arrive, of bureaucratic bungling that has driven honest citizens to suicide, or of food so disgusting even a dog wouldn't eat it (well, not an English dog).

English humour is as much about recognition as it is about their ability to laugh at themselves – 'I thought my mother was a rotten cook, but at least her gravy used to move about a bit.'

The wry smile that greets the well-judged understatement is a characteristic English expression. They love irony and expect others to appreciate it too, for example: One hill walker to another: 'It's only six miles by the map, yet your navigation made it ten.' 'Yes, but doing it in ten gives one a much greater feeling of accomplishment.'

A thick strand of ribaldry runs through much English comedy, as exemplified by the smut and 'earthiness' of Benny Hill and the '*Carry On...*' films, and the mimed humour of Mr Bean, while the richness of the English language lends itself to innuendo, and produces a characteristic English humorous device, the pun – as in:

'The pollution round here is terrible. You used to be able to swim in this bay – now you can only go through the motions.'

Obsessions

Homes...

It is largely thanks to the variable climate in England that the English lavish so much attention on their homes and gardens. They employ their leisure hours with an endless cycle of 'home improvements' without which no home can ever be considered fully improved.

Inside and out they busy themselves installing electronic gadgets, showers, built-in furniture and turning the exterior of a suburban semi into a gothic nightmare of mullioned windows, stone-clad walls and studded front doors.

Even the suburban family car is not safe from DIY man's attentions. He drives his impeccably polished vehicle up on to ramps, which he buys from the DIY shop, and tinkers around underneath it for hours on end.

You might think that, with all this self-servicing, self-plumbing, self-decorating and improving, English skilled labourers would be out of a job or two. But this is not the case. Sooner or later, these experts have to be called in to make good the damage caused by the over-enthusiastic amateur.

Leaning back on their heels, pencils behind ears, glancing sideways and taking in long breaths between their teeth, they shake their heads. "Of course you've been fiddling with this, haven't you?" DIY man winces at 'fiddling', puts his hand ruefully into his back pocket and pays handsomely. It is tacitly understood that part of the fee buys the expert's discretion. For DIY man will still take the credit for the shower, the burglar alarm or the 'suping up' of the family saloon.

No disaster will ever convince the Englishman that any job is beyond him. Every job is a challenge and all challenges are to be met.

...and Gardens

Out in the garden, the English have no hesitation. They are surprisingly effective out-of-doors. Gardening is a national sport and 'green fingers' are a proudly borne English deformity.

Once they get going, something very strange happens. They temporarily lose their innate practical bias in favour of a purely personal expression. While other nations tinker with pots and potagers in an attempt to increase the foodstore and add a splash of colour, the English are landscaping – dreaming of grandiose sweeps of green, studded with plantations of exotic shrubs.

While the French content themselves with a sprinkling of mostly native plants, the English suburban garden is a riot of international flora – lilies from Tibet, wistaria from China and gunnera from Patagonia.

Garden centres thrive. Gardening magazines, books and television programmes endorse the idea that the whole business is effortless, and that anyone can propagate. So when the temperature indoors is below freezing, the seedlings and cuttings in the greenhouse luxuriate in tropical warmth. And all this in the smallest of properties: a garden or window box becomes a national park in the English imagination.

Up and down the land, a dedicated band of enthusiasts forsake camelias for cabbages and carrots which they cultivate on allotments (municipally owned land leased to urbanites). Some will wait half a lifetime to inherit one of these insalubrious little plots with their ramshackle sheds, for here they can play at being market gardeners all weekend.

For the English the first sound of spring is not really the song of the cuckoo, but the echo of the unprintable oath of the gardener who discovers that his lawn mower will not start. After that first primaeval shout, they are off. And so, throughout the summer while other people in the world are sitting outside their houses chatting, the English apply themselves to the horticultural labours of Hercules. They weed monstrous herbaceous borders, build palaeolithic rockeries, divert waters to prime fountains, nurture giant marrows for the annual village fête and dead-head acres of asters.

If they feel in need of a change, they will go and visit someone else's garden, returning home via the garden centre with another car bootful of plants, implements, plastic pond liners and compost.

Come rain or shine, but mostly come rain, the English mulch and prune their way through the year, rejoicing in the dignity of their labour.

Gnomes

The garden gnome is a peculiarly English phenomenon which gives a fascinating insight into the English character.

In English suburban gardens the coarse-fishing gnome wielding his little rod is a reminder not of some pagan past but of a secret time before the coming of adulthood, the very childhood the English had thought they had forgotten. Along with coy garden poetry, a laughably impractical sundial and an Enid Blyton-type name on the garden gate – 'Bide-a-Wee', 'Dunroamin', 'Kenada' (the home of Kenneth and Ada) or 'Olcote' (Our Little Corner of This Earth) – the gnome helps to create, in a private place, a private world in which the Englishman is just a great friendly giant.

Animals

It is an English maxim that a person who likes animals cannot be all bad. The English adore animals – all kinds of animals. They keep them, not, as other nations do, primarily to guard their property, for scientific interest or for status, but for company.

Animals, especially pets, are vital to English life because pet-owning is for many English people the closest they ever get to an emotional relationship with another being. They are not always very good at talking to each other, but they excel in conversation with their animals. They may not be successful at forming tactile bonds with their children, yet they continually chuck the chins of their lapdogs and whisper sweet nothings into their hairy ears. Pets accept all this without complaint and consequently enjoy an unrivalled position in the English affection.

Pet owners' homes are shrines to their animals. The best seats, the warmest spots, the choicest morsels are handed over to these household gods as a matter of course. The British spend around £1.7 billion annually on pet food, twice as much as the total market for tea and coffee.

Cats and dogs, parrots and guinea pigs are excused behaviour which if seen in the children of the household might well end in assault. They are deemed to be incapable of almost any misdemeanour. So when dog bites man, it is always man's fault, even if he is just a passer-by. The victim may be severely savaged but everyone in the vicinity will sympathize with the owner's disclaimer: "Fang wouldn't hurt a fly!"

Cruelty to animals is abhorred which is why, for example, the English who still ride to hounds convince themselves that the fox enjoys being hunted. While national health hospitals in run-down metropolitan areas close their wards, wounded hedgehogs are tenderly cared for in a hedgehog hospital. Meanwhile in the cause of kindness, hundreds of vicious farmed mink are let loose by crusading animal rights activists to ravage innocent animals.

A Nice Cup of Tea

Foreigners may scoff, marketing men may try to seduce with alternatives, but the English still carry on doggedly in their devotion to what they consider to be one of the few good things ever to come from elsewhere.

Whilst other people stiffen their sinews with something stronger, the English constitution merely demands tea. They have imbued it with almost mystical curative and comforting qualities. In moments of crisis, as a remedy for shock or just at a social gathering someone will suggest tea. It is probably their only addiction.

Tea to the average English man or woman usually means Indian tea. It is served with milk and sugar and the folklore surrounding its preparation is prodigious. First the teapot has to be heated. The tea, once made, has to be left to 'stand' and 'brew' – but not so long that it becomes 'stewed'. Cold milk is poured into the bottom of each cup and then tea is added either with the addition of water or, more normally, 'just as it comes' – neat and strong.

China tea is considered smarter and preparation rituals are similar, but milk is always added after the tea if it is taken at all. A slice of lemon is often substituted. Sugar goes in last.

In great English institutions tea brewed in vast urns like Russian samovars still often comes with milk and sugar already added. It should be approached with caution. The liquid that oozes out of this receptacle is best described as 'canteen tea' – the kind that stands up without a cup.

Eating and Drinking

On the whole, England has always been, culinarily speaking, unadventurous. The puritan backlash is ever present. 'Good plain cooking' and 'honest simple fare' continue to be highly regarded, with the clear implication that complicated and pretty dishes are neither good nor honest.

The writer Somerset Maugham observed that one could eat very well in England, simply by having breakfast three times a day. Although the great English home-cooked breakfast – a sizzling feast of bacon, eggs, sausages, grilled tomatoes, mushrooms, kidneys, kippers, and so on – has given way to a belief that instant coffee and cornflakes must be healthier, it is still available all day and night at motorway service stations.

Roast beef, lamb or pork with vegetables and roast potatoes are still the nation's favourite choice for 'a proper meal'. At all other times, and when inspiration fails, the English fall back on their other traditional dish of baked beans on toast.

Potatoes form an important constituent of the main meal of the day. The average person gets through two hundredweight (100 kilos) of them every year. Much of this is in the form of crispy snacks and, of course, chips – with fish, burgers, and other fried foods – or just on their own with salt and vinegar. They are even enjoyed in the form of 'chip butties', stuffed between two halves of a buttered bun.

Most people wouldn't consider a meal finished unless they had a pudding – steamed jam roll, rhubarb crumble, apple pie, treacle pudding, strawberry tart – all from the freezer cabinet. The unwary should take care with 'Yorkshire' and 'black' puddings. Neither is quite what it seems. The first is baked batter eaten with roast beef, and the second a ferocious blood sausage.

As the interest in foreign food has grown, so have the choices. The supremacy of French and Italian fare is now challenged by others – Thai, Chinese, Mexican, Spanish, Russian, American. There are even restaurants specialising in English food. One highly successful example in London calls itself 'School Dinners'. There tired and over-wrought businessmen can enjoy such old-fashioned fare as bread and butter pudding and 'spotted dick', all served by well-developed girls wearing school uniforms.

In spite of their tastes becoming more sophisticated, the English still treasure the sandwich. Having invented it, they were once content with no more than a cheese and chutney filling, but these days the designer sandwich can contain anything from smoked salmon and cream cheese to chicken Tikka Masala.

English taste is insidious. It assimilates all who come into contact with it. Only in England would an Indian restaurant happily sell chips with curry sauce. Only the English would eat them.

The Pub

The traditional English town pub is divided into two bars, like First and Second class on the railways. The Saloon (or Lounge) Bar, haunt of travelling salesmen and 'Ladies', has a nylon carpet, chintzy furnishings, fake horse brasses and higher prices. The Public Bar has darts, bar billiards or pool, one–armed bandits and better service; it is for ordinary people and women.

The village pub is a classless institution dating back several centuries. It usually has one bar plus a 'snug' or small restaurant. In many places it is the focal point of the community, a cross between a social club, a citizens' advice bureau and a parliament, and class and social distinctions are left outside. It has been observed that you could go to any village pub in England, and ask "Is the Major in?" and the answer would be either, "He's in the snug," or "You've just missed him."

Lager and bottled Continental and American beers are popular, especially among the young, who tend to drink in 'theme bars', but the traditional English pint which once seemed on the brink of extinction has undergone a renaissance. Thanks to the efforts of the Campaigners for Real Ale (a quintessentially English organisation devoted to the preservation, encouragement and consumption of traditional brews), a brimming glass of unfizzy, unchilled, hop-scented beer, hand pumped from a wooden barrel in the cellar is increasingly available in all its glorious regional and local variations.

The habit of drinking 'rounds' is responsible for perhaps two-thirds of pub sales. It is not the done thing to drink with others without buying your round. The advantage is that only one person needs to leave the group in order to get six drinks instead of six people queuing up individually. The disadvantage is that you can end up drinking six pints when you only came in for one.

What is Sold Where

Until a few years ago everyone used to shop at their local greengrocer, butcher, baker and so on. Now these small shops have all but capitulated as their customers pile into their cars and get everything they need at huge out-of-town-centre hangars filled with all their hearts' desires.

Having once survived the march of the giant chains, even the corner shops are in crises because the enterprising Asians who ran them have moved on to do their MBAs. These shops are often supermarkets in miniature and sell anything from sweets to sweat bands, nappies to newspapers. Many of them are also open all day and half the night.

In all this cultural upheaval, there appears to be only one golden rule. You can get anything you need in very small or very big shops and nothing in medium-sized ones.

Health and Hygiene

The French are fascinated by their livers, the Germans by their digestive systems and the Spanish by their blood. To the English, none of these have anything like the appeal of the bowels.

From earliest childhood, the English are brought up to take a keen interest in the regularity and consistency of their bowel movements. The day that does not start with a satisfactory visit to the lavatory starts on the wrong foot. It is a preoccupation that lasts for life.

While their Continental neighbours breakfast on pastries and jam, the English tuck into bowls of cereal, rich in fibre and advertising their efficacy through such names as 'Force' or 'All Bran'. Correctives for bowel disorders throng English bathroom shelves and old-fashioned remedies continue to sell well. 'Carter's Little Liver Pills' promise to cure 'that out-of-sorts feeling due to constipation'. 'Syrup of Figs' is billed as an effective laxative for all the family. Both are less violent and unpleasant than their no-nonsense rival, good old-fashioned Castor Oil.

Over-enthusiasm in correcting the effects of being 'bound up' can lead to 'looseness' for which there is yet another array of proprietary medicines designed to bring one back to an acceptably solid state.

Kept reasonably steady on home ground, English bowels suffer exquisitely abroad. Thanks to the appalling nature of local food and water, the intrepid traveller constantly runs into problems. From 'Delhi Belly' to 'Montezuma's Revenge' or 'The Aztec Quickstep' they strike him or her in every far-flung corner of the earth.

Many juggle with purgatives and binding agents all their lives in the hope of one day returning to that blissful childhood state when an adult would nod approvingly at the first droppings of the day. For them this faecal nirvana is never reached. None of them can be persuaded to flirt with the ubiquitous suppository so beloved of the

Europeans. While the French will even treat a headache with one, the English would rather doctor themselves with potions and prunes.

With more serious illnesses, the English are at their most stoic. Fortitude in the face of adversity is the thing. Remember Queen Victoria's dying words: 'I feel a little better...'

Hygiene

When it comes to hygiene, the English are traditionally inclined. Showers are gaining in popularity but in most houses the bath still reigns supreme. Here the English will happily wallow in their own dirt, diluted with warm, soapy water.

The average household gets through more soap and deodorants than any other Europe nation. This, as far as they are concerned, counts for a lot. For as every English person knows, other nations, especially the French, just put on more scent when they start to smell.

Leisure and Pleasure

In English eyes, leisure activities share with sport the element of competition so essential to the English way of life. Leisure is a challenge and one must make one's own better than anyone else's.

The high-flying executive who plays with model helicopters on the Common is subconsciously waiting for another high flier with similar toys to compete with. The man who cleans his car in a suburban street on a Sunday morning is really running a polishing race with his neighbours with every grunting sweep of the chamois leather. Even a peaceful pint in the pub can easily turn into a drinking competition if the right adversary turns up.

This test-to-destruction principle even extends to theme parks. The passive consumerism of Disneyland is not for the English. Sensible and cautious they may be most of the time, but in a theme park they reveal themselves as closet thrill-seekers. The ideal is one which offers a simulacrum of skydiving, potholing, bobsleighing and white-water racing all rolled into one SAS-style assault course, and the ancient practice of queuing is indulged to its fullest extent for such delights as 'Deathdive', 'Nemesis', Suicide Ride' and 'You Must Be Completely Bonkers To Want A Go On This One'.

A close cousin of the theme park is the safari park, an attempt by impoverished aristocrats to keep their creditors at bay by populating their estates with large predatory African mammals and charging people to drive their cars around in the hope of seeing one. Large notices warn visitors to keep their windows shut; most English people respond by leaving them just a little bit open, to allow the possibility of being just a little bit mauled.

The Challenge

When bad weather threatens, the English, unlike other people, do not invariably take shelter in their houses. For heavy weather is the ultimate adversary – a worthy and familiar opponent. Wrapped from head to foot in water-proof clothing, they set out on extended hikes, best feet forward, carrying maps in little plastic bags around their necks. Up hill and down dale, the English follow vehemently protected footpaths on these route marches which they deceptively refer to as 'rambles'.

Uncomfortable forays of this kind are a particular favourite. In summer months they will travel miles to such places as the Grimpen Mire or the Lake District where rain can be almost guaranteed, to pit their stamina against the worst that nature can throw at them.

So popular are these struggles against the elements that some enterprising individuals have formulated courses in physical discomfort in remote and inhospitable areas where people pay substantial fees to be assured of a serious challenge. These courses, posing under such romantic titles as 'Survival', are pursued for their perceived character-building qualities. The stiffening of upper lips is guaranteed.

Companies, sparing no expense, will send their executives away for days on end to play these games. The assumption is that anyone who can shine in physical adversity will also excel in stressful business struggles. It does not seem to occur to them to sack all their employees and take on the men who run the courses instead.

Sports

The nation's most popular participation sport is fishing – which the English always refer to as 'angling' because it sounds as though some skill may be required to do it. More people fish than play football.

But the Englishman's true devotion to sport lies in watching other people play it. Watching sport provides a vent for all his pent-up emotions as well as the comfort of tribal solidarity. Vast numbers of soccer fans will sit up all night with bags of crisps and bags under their eyes to watch the 44th repeat of a goal being scored. Even if they cannot afford to pay for TV sports channels, they will ensure their children have their team's new strip regardless of the cost or how many times it changes.

Hard-core supporters will show up in the flesh to barrack the opposition in spectator stands or from touch-lines, often in sub-zero temperatures or force ten gales with the ever-present threat of a downpour. Nothing can dampen their ardour.

The average football fan is inured to failure and even derives a sort of masochistic pleasure from his team's ability to snatch defeat – or if he's lucky, a nil-nil draw – from the jaws of victory. The exception is the Manchester United supporter who expects his team to win everything all the time and whinges bitterly when it doesn't. Manchester United has the biggest following of any football club in the world. Each issue of the club's magazine sells in vast numbers – 30,000 copies alone in Taiwan.

Cricket

Cricket to the English is not just a game. It is a symbol – a 22-man personification of all English beliefs and philosophies. Ignore it at your peril. If you do you could be 'on a sticky wicket'. You might then be accused of not having put your 'best foot forward' and of not 'playing a straight bat', both hallmarks of the bounder.

Cricket is alleged to be the national summer pastime of the English race. People who are interested in it are passionate about it, but those who are not are totally indifferent to it. Visitors to England would have to be blind not to spot at least one weekend cricket match in their travels. And even the blind cannot avoid the coverage of international matches which dribbles out of radios in every public place throughout the season. It is inescapable. On every village green or television screen, groups of men, dressed in white, stand around waiting for something to happen.

The English invented cricket 750 years ago and are fiercely proprietorial about it. Its laws are one of the great mysteries of life, passed on among the initiated in a coded language. In the past they took the game all over the world and always won. But gradually other nations' teams have got better at it, until now the English stand a pretty safe chance of being beaten wherever they go.

Whenever this happens, the English get very heated. They accuse everyone in sight of having cheated: of tampering with the ball by roughing up the surface (so that it behaves in an irregular fashion); of shaving the head (to reduce wind-resistance on the run-in); of 'sledging' (hurling abuse at the batsman so as to put him off his stroke); of 'intimidatory bowling' (aiming at the batsman rather than the wicket) and of playing too fast for a one-day match – all of which they vigorously complain is just 'not cricket', unless, of course, they are at it themselves.

Having a Flutter

Entering a betting shop (or 'turf accountant') produces the same sort of frisson as visiting a speakeasy in 1920s Chicago. The English gaming laws decree that the shameful goings-on inside must not be visible from the street, so the windows are frosted or painted out and the open doorway obscured with stripey plastic strips. The interior is dim and bare, with no tables and nothing to sit on; a narrow shelf at chest height is used to write bets on, and to lean against in gloomy anticipation of their outcome. The floor serves as an ashtray. The betting shop is the perfect illustration of the English tradition of taking one's pleasure unpleasurably. Disappointment at backing a loser is tempered with relief at not having to go back there to collect one's winnings.

Contrastingly, a day out at the races, particularly in the carnival atmosphere of one of the 'classics' such as the Grand National or the Derby, is almost unmitigatedly enjoyable.

Annual Holidays

Once a year most English families take an extended holiday. Until air travel became more common these family holidays were almost always spent in one of the many coastal seaside resorts. During July and August convoys of Austins, Rovers and Fords would snake their way down winding English lanes to seaside towns. Here shops on the seafront sold buckets, spades, lilos, risqué postcards, candyfloss, toffee apples, sticks of rock, and fish and chips.

Pitching their camps of brightly coloured canvas wind breaks on the beach, English families spent days on end appearing to enjoy melting ice creams, leaking thermos flasks and sand in everything.

Nowadays the English start their holidays at Gatwick, Stansted, Luton, Manchester, Birmingham or Heathrow airports and fly over those winding English lanes, bound for Spain, Greece, Cyprus, Florida or anywhere sunny where they can still be guaranteed amusement arcades, risqué postcards to send home, and the reassuring smell of fried food.

There many carry on just as if they were still in Bognor, Blackpool or Brighton. They stick together, ignoring the existence of the natives, stake out corners of the beach and spend most of the day lying in the sun. At night they drink, dance, and throw up in discotheques thoughtfully provided for the purpose by the locals.

These are the kind of English holiday-makers who only feel they have had a proper holiday if – with peeling noses, runny tummies and alcohol poisoning – they return home feeling as though they need one.

Culture

England is the country of Shakespeare, Milton, Byron, Dickens and Beatrix Potter. The first is, by common consent, a hero of the human race, a Titan of literature against whom all other writers in the world over the past 400 years have been measured. The second three are worthy names in most literate households. But the work of the fourth is best known; for while the others tended to write about people, Beatrix Potter wrote about animals.

So it is that a mention of Peter Rabbit, Mrs Tiggy-Winkle and Jeremy Fisher elicit an immediate response from English audiences while the agonies of Hamlet, Coriolanus and Othello leave the better read of them intellectually stimulated but emotionally stone-cold.

Other nations may thrill to Henry V's call to arms at Agincourt or warm to Juliet's tearful pleas to her Romeo, but English audiences of all ages reach for the tissues on hearing how Jemima Puddleduck outwits the fox, adjusts her bonnet and escapes the cooking pot to live another sunny day. Close on the heels of Beatrix Potter comes A.A. Milne, whose *Winnie-The-Pooh* – written by an adult for other adults but passed off as a children's book – is read by adults for the rest of their lives.

Anthropomorphic juvenilia apart, the English cherish their literary culture mostly by ignoring it. They treat it as they treat their best tea service: it's nice to know it's there, but one would never dream of actually *using* it.

Television

For the majority of English, watching television is their only real experience of a broader 'culture'. They are world leaders in video culture – with more cassette recorders than any other nation.

English television, naturally, majors in sports coverage

and heroic struggles occur between television companies to win exclusive rights to televise the most popular events. But even the English cannot quite live by sport alone. Pandering to the competitive nature of their audiences, broadcasters screen large numbers of quiz and games shows. In addition they produce a wealth of news and discussion programmes and the occasional original drama series. These are bulked out with a staggering number of imported and specially created soap operas and mini-series, which are hugely popular. For the rest, it is old films of which the English never tire.

Programmes aimed at the more intellectual members of society are screened late at night so as to cause the least inconvenience to the majority.

The Press

The average Frenchman travelling to work reads a novel, the English read newspapers. Their voracious appetite for printed news, gossip and scandal is unequalled and the English newspaper market has attracted entrepreneurs from all over the world who struggle to the death to obtain the proprietorship of one of the chunks of it.

Nobody really understands why. The press cannot hope to compete for immediacy of coverage with radio and television. Perhaps it is because the English prefer their news, like their climate – cold. Or perhaps it is because they secretly believe that anything viewed in retrospect is really more real. Or perhaps they just like doing the crosswords.

The Arts

The English theatre today is mainly supported by block bookings for new productions of old musicals or for the latest Andrew Lloyd Webber spectacular. These the

English will pay for. When Lloyd Webber meets Beatrix Potter, nobody will be able to get a seat.

With the cinema, things are a little more encouraging. Rumours of its total demise 30 years ago turned out to have been somewhat exaggerated, and even foreign films are seen by thousands in cinemas every week. But then the English do love an 'outing'.

Dragging their children behind them they will visit museums and art galleries to rub shoulders with foreign visitors and buy souvenirs and reproductions of famous paintings. When it comes to art appreciation, they tend to be nervous, suspecting that they are not all that good at it. On the whole they show a marked preference for large paintings of people and animals by artists like Landseer. If the picture tells a story, so much the better. If they cannot understand it, they tend to dismiss it.

Fundamentally, the English see themselves more in the role of patrons than of artists. For most of them culture is a luxury and too much luxury is a dangerous thing.

Custom

Family Gatherings

Though they are the least family-orientated people on earth, the English would not dream of spending their Christmas anywhere else but in the vipers' nest they refer to as the 'bosom of the family'. This annual festival almost always ends in tears and to get over it takes many families a good six months. But tradition rules and, come October, English families are beginning to plan for another family Christmas, having apparently completely forgotten the mayhem of the one before.

Christmas apart, family members avoid each other religiously throughout the year except on compulsory occasions such as christenings, weddings and funerals. Of these, christenings and funerals, being the shortest, are the most popular. Weddings are only distinguishable from pitched battles by the uniforms of the participants.

Planning for these nightmare events starts early, as do the arguments. Even though English etiquette books try to help by pointing out who is responsible for organising and paying for the bride's dress, the flowers, the church, the choir, the organist, the cars, the reception, the food, the photographers and St John's Ambulance, the English will fight furiously on every single issue for months before, right through and even after the great day.

It came as no surprise to many survivors of similar occasions to read the newspaper report of the bride's father who initiated legal proceedings against his son-in-law's parents about who should pay what, while the 'happy couple' were still on their honeymoon.

It is the triumph of English hope over English experience that these gatherings ever take place at all.

Guy Fawkes

On 5th November the English let off fireworks and set fire to vast mounds of rubbish while they burn the effigy of someone who tried to blow up the Houses of Parliament in 1606. His foiled attempt is celebrated not because he was discovered before he could kill the King (who was hugely unpopular), but because he was stopped in the nick of time from disrupting the status quo.

Systems

Public Transport

It is a tradition that trains generally do not run on time unless the passenger is two minutes late. It is also a tradition that, although the price of railway travel is infinitely variable, concessionary rates are only available at times or days other than those on which one wishes to travel.

Urban buses travel in convoys so as to ensure that passengers wait as long as possible at the bus stops. Then, just before fighting breaks out among the waiting hordes, three or four buses sporting the same number will heave into view. It is always a feast or a famine.

Whatever transport you choose you will find that, in England, you are nearly always late. This is because, contrary to popular belief, the English are not punctual by nature. It is considered polite to arrive at least 15 minutes after the time you were invited for. English transport will probably ensure that you do anyhow. It's all part of the system.

The Not So Open Road

Almost everyone over the age of 17 either owns or has access to a car and uses it frequently, especially for short journeys in suburban areas. This leads to enormous traffic and parking problems in towns and to terminal motorway congestion. The average speed in built-up areas is now 11 miles an hour – slower than driving a horse and carriage a hundred years ago.

The English resent an unmended road, and their highways are under constant siege as vast stretches are cordoned off behind lines of red and white cones. Commuters with time to spare can call a special 'cones hotline' to keep track of the exact geographical location of these no-go areas. Whole communities with Portakabins, Portaloos and car parks of their own spring up as road menders are joined by men working for the gas, electricity, water, telephone and cable TV companies. More often than not this happens serially. When the last of them folds his tent, it's time for the road-menders to move in again.

Driving on the left is traditional and therefore, to the English, indisputably right. The custom dates back to the time when the horse was the main means of getting about, and you kept to the left so as to leave your sword arm free to defend yourself. Nowadays it is more usually extended through the open window to reinforce the helpful hints offered to other motorists.

The English are remarkably well-behaved on the roads. They use their horns sparingly and often give way to each other at crossroads. Punctilious in their observation of traffic signs, they will wait at traffic-light-controlled pedestrian crossings even if there are no pedestrians in sight. If there are any, they screech to a halt and wait patiently for them to cross the road. This comes as a surprise to foreigners who are used to crossing themselves on the pavement before running like rabbits across the highway.

A Good Education

For English children whose parents can afford it, school often means a public (which really means private) school and frequently means boarding. The parents of pupils at public schools approve of boarding. They believe that children develop better away from home.

Although there are some mixed public schools, many are single-sex establishments, where pupils have the opportunity of experiencing some aspects of the monastic or prison existence at an early stage in their lives.

The alternative is the State system with its free public (which really means public) day schools. These suffer from a periodic shortage of teachers (bad pay), equipment and stationery (lack of funds), pupils (truancy) and buildings (set alight and vandalised). They are also afflicted with a constant change in educational philosophy.

Whether public or private, the concern is still for 'a good education', the feeling being that life and all its possibilities will thereafter be yours for the asking. However, like so many things in the English way of life 'you get what you pay for'. The implication is clear. If you are not paying, you are not getting much.

Crime and Punishment

The English 'bobby' on the beat who can be asked the way or the time and who will always give a civil answer really does exist. Unlike their counterparts in other countries, the police prefer to rely for their own protection not on a gun but a two-way radio, a CS spray-can and a retractable truncheon.

Serried ranks of them attend every open-air occasion and provide a comforting sense of support. They are always on hand everywhere except, as the English observe, when you really need one.

People expect their police to be beyond reproach and are shocked to the core when charges of brutality or corruption come to light, despite the fact that such behaviour is the stuff of many police dramas on television. As far as the English are concerned, life should never imitate art.

Official figures for reported crime are reassuring. Only 4.6% of English adults are the victims of theft, 2.55% of burglary, and 0.75% of violent crime, while 0.01% of the population are murdered. On the other hand, thefts involving cars add up to some 1.3 million annually, the highest rate in Europe. Figures for *un*reported crime are even less comforting. They suggest, for example, that one-third of the victims of theft, burglary and vandalism don't bother to report the crime as they don't think the police would be interested, or able to do anything about it, while 47% of assault victims claim to have 'dealt with the matter themselves'.

The ability of the police to clear up crime is variable: 93% of murders are solved, but only around 26% of reported crimes generally. Cynics suggest this as the reason why so many of the police seem to spend their lives randomly stopping motorists by the hundred thousand, in the hope of finding a few who might have drunk too much.

Much of the emphasis of modern policing is on crime prevention, with great success being claimed for security video cameras in public places, particularly when someone hasn't forgotten to put a tape in them. Forty shoplifters a month were caught in Romford, Essex, until a new surveillance initiative banned prosecuted offenders from entering the town. Crime plummeted. This was good news for Romford but bad news for neighbouring Upminster where traders reported that the shoplifters had moved in on them.

Prison

The English have problems with prisons. They have only just woken up to the reality of an overcrowded, squalid and crumbling system. Recent reforms have improved matters: the installation of lavatories in cells has at last put an end to the practice known as 'slopping-out', but the overcrowding remains, and redundant ships have been pressed into service to act as prison hulks.

Another problem is that they can't decide what prison is for: whether simply to keep bad people out of circulation, or 'reform' them, or give them a really horrible time. The public's reaction is one of outrage at reports that prisons are like 'luxury hotels', or that drugs are more freely available inside than out, or that some well publicised criminal has 'got away' with community service instead of incarceration. The latest solution has been to privatise prisons and hand them over to American 'Correctional Facilitators' to run. The English find the shortcomings of Americans much easier to analyse.

Law

English law, like many aspects of English life, is based on precedent. This means that everything is decided on what has been decided before.

The right to be tried, in all criminal cases, before a jury of one's equals forms the basis of Common law. In such cases, guilt can only be established if proved 'beyond reasonable doubt' otherwise one is assumed to be innocent (or at any rate not criminally guilty). The English like to think that the presumption of innocence shows what a jolly nice, trusting lot they all are.

This is all most people know (or care) about their law; the rest is largely impenetrable to the average citizen.

In the criminal courts, the law is acted out as real-life drama in period costume as the judiciary, the guilty and the innocent juggle with truth and falsehood in a courageous attempt to find either. And then, if a prisoner's guilt is established, to make the punishment fit the crime. It is the proud boast of the English legal system that this sometimes happens.

Government and Bureaucracy

The Constitution

The English like to believe they are ruled by consent. Whatever the realities of the situation, they have to feel that they are the masters of their own fate. They do not take kindly to control of any sort and insist on the fiction that they do so only on a voluntary basis.

The English Constitution, which formed the bedrock of the British one when the parts of the UK were incorporated, is largely an unwritten one, based on an accumulation of customs, conventions and laws. As with so much else, things happen the way they do because that is the way they have always happened.

The English are proud of the fact that they have no Bill of Rights for individual citizens. Being English, why should they need one? They point out that having a list of things you can't do leaves plenty of scope for the imaginative citizen to dream up things the authorities haven't got round to making illegal; whereas having a list of things you can do (as in America) leaves the authorities plenty of scope to find reasons for locking you up.

The Monarchy

Contrary to the popular belief that supporting a monarch is a hugely expensive business, the British royal family costs each UK citizen no more than 6p per year to support – a bargain compared with the expense of impeaching a President.

The Monarch is not only the social supremo, but Head of the Church and titular Head of Government. Tax demands come in an envelope printed 'On Her Majesty's Service' and even the mail is Royal. The head of the monarch on every postage stamp (with no mention of a country of origin) is unique to Britain. This is not because the British think the world knows and recognises the profile of their Queen on each postage stamp, but simply because they invented it.

Government

Parliament is divided into two houses, the Commons (directly elected) and the Lords (awarded and inherited), though changes are in motion to abolish the appointment of hereditary peers in the Lords. This is considered most unfair by those whom it will affect, not because they will lose their voting rights but because they will no longer have membership of the club.

Outside Parliament, government is shared between County, Borough, District, Town and Parish Councils, all of whom receive about 80% of their funding from central funds and raise the rest through local taxes – and their ability to run local affairs the way they would like to is a reflection of this.

The English have an ambivalent attitude to bureaucracy. They know it's a necessary evil but their natural instinct for directness and individuality means that they object to its interference. But on one thing they are unanimous: English red tape may be invasive, but it is definitely boulevards ahead of anything the Continent has to offer.

Politics

The populace know that politicians are out for their own ends and not to be trusted, yet Ministers are expected to be models of rectitude and if they cannot manage that, they are expect to do the decent thing – resign.

Deep down the English are a conservative bunch and do not like change, which is just as well because they seldom get it. In the Mother of Parliaments at

Westminster (in a building designed in the 19th century to look 500 years old) their politicians carry on their business with much historical pageantry and partially in period costume.

It is no surprise that the political scene is dominated by two parties not called Republicans, Christian Democrats, Solidarity or any other inflated names, but Conservative and Labour. The former echoes the unchanging quality of English life. The latter, the Puritan work ethic with its dignification of labour for its own sake. Adding 'New' to the word Labour simply changed a pugnacious proletarian party to a politically correct conservative party under another name.

The rebranding of the third-party Liberals, once one of the 'big two', as the Liberal Democrats led to a doubling of their representation in Parliament. Not so long ago, you could fit their MPs into a taxicab. Now, you would need a bus, though not yet a double-decker.

Business

Getting By

To the rest of the world English business people still have a somewhat amateur air. They seem to prefer to rely on an instinctive approach to business, mistrusting foreign methods of analysis and working. This makes them slightly out of their depth in the global business arena.

In business practice operations are characterised by an unusual devotion to democracy. Almost every decision is taken by committee. So much so, that whenever you try to get hold of an English business man or woman, you will invariably be told that he or she is 'in a meeting'. Here they will sit trying to reach consensus in preference to a decision.

The popularly held belief that the English work harder than other people took a hammering when a report showed that, on average, the Germans work 44.9 hours a week, the Italians 42.4 and the English 42. The English, of course, pointed out that both the Germans and the Italians have more holidays and that, anyhow, it is not the quantity but the quality of work that counts.

They pride themselves fiercely on their ability to 'muddle through', that is to act without too much worry about discipline or planning. In the past this attitude has served them well, and the past holds all the lessons the English wish to learn.

In Good Company

Companies are still largely organised on traditional lines. That is to say, they are based on the concept of a many layered pyramid – a vertical chain of command from the Chairman and Managing Director at the top to the humblest employee at the bottom.

Some things don't change. A survey of university graduates found that those from independent (private) schools still get better-paid jobs than their state-educated peers. The traditional 'old boy network' may have been shaken, but it remains unstirred. An old school tie is still a good investment.

Just Obeying Orders

Because the English do not like being told what to do, any order has to be given with a degree of politeness which many other nations find incomprehensible.

Should you follow custom and express an order as a request, you will achieve the desired effect. Express it simply as an order, with no hint of personal choice, and the English will invariably break for tea.

Time Keeping

On the whole, the English admire punctuality and aim for it, but not obsessively. Time can be measured in very small amounts: 'Half a mo' is smaller than 'a sec' but not quite as small as 'just a tick'. On the other hand, 'hang on a minute' can mean anything up to five or six, and 'give me five minutes' usually means around 15. (Public clocks subscribe to the democratic principle of dividing the time between them, each one giving its own approximation of the same quarter hour.)

Language

The English are inordinately proud of their language, even though most of them use only a tiny bit of it (often badly). The *Complete Oxford Dictionary* runs to 23 volumes and contains over 500,000 words. German, on the other hand, has a vocabulary of about 185,000 and French fewer than 100,000. Shakespeare had a working vocabulary of 30,000 words (some of which he made up), twice that of a modern, educated English person. Most of the English manage on around 8,000 – the same as the King James Bible.

English began as a basic means for various tribes to communicate with each other without all the fuss of gender and inflections, and the secret of its success is that, like the English themselves, it has gone on assimilating from every other culture it has come into contact with, from Arabic ('algebra') to Yiddish ('nosh'). No other language has so many ways of saying almost the same thing.

The English approve of this tradition of change, while at the same time disapproving of change itself, which they blame (often wrongly) on the Americans – until they get used to it and regard it as Standard English. They like to dispute its usage ('compare with' or 'to'), its pronunciation ('harass', 'controversy'), and its spelling ('miniscule', 'extravert'). It's a game they take very seriously.

Meanwhile, English is to communication what Microsoft is to computing: the world cannot do without it. The French may insist that its use in aviation is 'pending the development and adoption of a more suitable form of expression', but it marches on regardless. One billion people use it; 80% of the Internet and 75% of the world's mail is written in it, and 200 million-odd Chinese at any given moment are learning it. India has more native English speakers than England has. The Voyager 1 spacecraft in deep space beyond the solar system carries a message from the United Nations on behalf of 147 countries – in English.

It will soon be possible for English people to travel anywhere in the world and speak their own language without having to repeat themselves or raise their voices. It's a prospect which makes them feel – in a word which has no exact equivalent in any of the world's other 2,700 languages or cultures – comfy.

Conversation and Gestures

In conversation the English are at their most obtuse for they hardly ever say what they mean, and very often say the exact opposite. Thus when you are telling a story which elicits the response "How interesting", it should not be taken at face value. Faint praise damns as surely as criticism.

When one person enquires about the health of another, the response will invariably be "Mustn't grumble!" This is English hypocrisy writ large. For grumbling is a national pastime. In conversation they love to find fault and no aspect of their lives escapes a moan – their health, the Government, bureaucracy, the price of food, young people, old people – all are grist to their mill. Nodding sagely and united in discontent, they lay into anything and everything. And finally, refreshed by a good groaning session, they accept the unlikelihood of anything actually happening to improve the situation with the grumbler's amen – "Typical!"

Conversational Triggers

Because conversation does not come easily to the English, they have developed a bewildering battery of metaphors with which everyone is familiar and comfortable. These include euphemisms for the avoidance of verbal confrontation with 'tricky' subjects. Thus the English do not die, they 'pass over', 'pass on', 'pop off', 'kick the bucket', 'give up the ghost' or 'snuff it'. When they relieve themselves they 'spend a penny', 'wash their hands', 'answer the call' or, simply, 'go'.

They are devoted to a huge range of hackneyed expressions which they drag out frequently to keep the conversational ball in play or to cover their escape. Because they are slightly ashamed of the triteness of these, they refer to them dismissively in French as 'clichés'. Moving from one to another, the skilful user will defy categorisation and avoid taking a stance on any subject under discussion.

To the English many such phrases are so familiar that they are not usually quoted in full. Meteorological clichés are particularly familiar and, as such, never completed. So "it's an ill wind...", "it never rains...", "every cloud..."* and so on tumble one upon the other and only the English know just how little they all really mean.

*'...that blows no good'; '...but it pours'; '...has a silver lining'.

Niceness

'Nice' is the most overworked word in the English language whose meaning can only be divined by its context.

Being essentially non-specific and uncontentious, it can be used on any occasion to convey a response generally tending towards non-committal approval of anything from the weather to working practices. Its negative form – 'not very nice' – describes habits as diverse as nose-picking to cannibalism.

The English grow up with 'nice'. As children they are warned off antisocial behaviour with the reprimand "Nice boys (or girls) don't do that!" and by the time they totter into their first conversations, they can use the word with deadly effect. They may even imitate their elders by using it sarcastically – a favourite ploy – to put down bad behaviour: "That's nice! That's very nice!", when the tone of voice says it all. Sarcasm is very much part of the English conversational stock in trade.

English Weather

Without the topic of the weather, the English would be without one of the most useful weapons in their conversational armoury.

Rather like the inhabitants, the weather in the British Isles is particularly unpredictable. The geographic location of the country makes it naturally prey to momentary atmospheric changes, and forward planning of any outdoor event is fraught with dangers.

The English have, of course, lived with this situation for hundreds of years but, not being extreme themselves, extremes in weather conditions always take them by surprise. So, if it snows, the country's transport systems grind instantly to a halt while negotiations are made to import snow-ploughs from abroad. In the spring, flash flooding drives householders on to their roofs to unblock their gutters, and the innocent falling leaves of autumn frequently cause the railways to seize up completely.

But while late frosts kill cherished plants and cloud-bursts wash away the tea tents at village fêtes in high summer, they have, in English eyes, a higher purpose – to furnish conversation. "Nippy, isn't it?", "They say it'll be sunny tomorrow", "Looks like we're in for a cold snap". Bracing, parky, muggy, nippy, breezy, crisp, chilly, fresh, balmy – conditions are always understated by at least 10 degrees. The weather is not just their preferred conversational topic, it is their favourite gap-filler. When you can tell the difference between 'scattered showers', 'showery outbreaks', and 'intermittent rain', you'll know you have finally arrived at a state of complete Englishness.

Gestures

The use of hand gestures in communication is viewed with deep suspicion. Fluttering hands and supple wrists are sure signs of theatricality (insincerity), effeminacy or foreign extraction. English hands are usually kept firmly to English sides in all conversation. But they should be in sight at all times. It is considered very bad manners to talk to anyone with the hands in the pockets, as if preparing an instrument of aggression or silently counting loose change.

People will usually only use hand gestures when they are absolutely necessary, such as for pointing the way (index finger of the right hand extended) or for making a forceful suggestion (index and middle fingers of the right hand raised in a 'V'). This offensive gesture was first employed by English archers at Agincourt when standing just beyond the reach of the enemy's arrows. They used it to indicate that they still had their bow fingers which if they were captured, the French would cut off. It's the ultimate replacement for words.

The Authors

Antony Miall was born in the Lake District but migrated south at the age of nine months. He spent his childhood in Royal Tunbridge Wells where he had ample opportunity to observe the English at their most characteristic.

Apart from a brief spell in an educational establishment in one of the northern home counties, he has spent his life safely south of the Thames within easy reach of the South of France. This suits him very well because he has never quite qualified in Englishness. Among the subjects he is unable to get to grips with are discomfort and moderation.

In addition to shopping, his enthusiasms include playing the piano better than he thought he could. He also enjoys seeing his name in print and has written several books on Victorian songs and society. Now a public relations consultant, his clients have included the manufacturer of water beds for convalescent dogs.

Once happily married, he is now just happily in Wandsworth, has one daughter, three cats and a very significant other.

David Milsted, a typically mongrel Englishman (in his case, one-quarter Scots with trace elements of Viking), was born in Sussex in 1954 and subsequently drifted northwards, eventually spending 15 years on various Scottish islands before relocating, more or less accidentally, in Dorset, where he and his four sons constitute a 0.75% typical English family.

A former teacher, fireman and postman, he is now a full-time writer, researcher and editor who makes occasional forays into broadcasting, the theatre, and the strangely beautiful world of corporate malt whisky tasting. He has published four novels and a number of other books, the latest being *The Cassell Dictionary of Regrettable Quotations*.